KIDS SPEAK OUT About

VIOLENCE

#StopAbuse

Kids for Peace! MAKE A CHANGE!

HOPE

KIDS CARE!

TAKE ACTION

#SpeakUp

CHRIS SCHWAB

Rourke
Educational Media

A Division of
Carson
Dellosa
Education

BEFORE AND DURING READING ACTIVITIES

Before Reading: *Building Background Knowledge and Vocabulary*

Building background knowledge can help children process new information and build upon what they already know. Before reading a book, it is important to tap into what children already know about the topic. This will help them develop their vocabulary and increase their reading comprehension.

Questions and Activities to Build Background Knowledge:

1. Look at the front cover of the book and read the title. What do you think this book will be about?
2. What do you already know about this topic?
3. Take a book walk and skim the pages. Look at the table of contents, photographs, captions, and bold words. Did these text features give you any information or predictions about what you will read in this book?

Vocabulary: *Vocabulary Is Key to Reading Comprehension*

Use the following directions to prompt a conversation about each word.

- Read the vocabulary words.
- What comes to mind when you see each word?
- What do you think each word means?

> ### Vocabulary Words:
> - abuse
> - demanded
> - drills
> - physically
> - protest
> - refugee
> - survived
> - victims

During Reading: *Reading for Meaning and Understanding*

To achieve deep comprehension of a book, children are encouraged to use close reading strategies. During reading, it is important to have children stop and make connections. These connections result in deeper analysis and understanding of a book.

 Close Reading a Text

During reading, have children stop and talk about the following:

- Any confusing parts
- Any unknown words
- Text to text, text to self, text to world connections
- The main idea in each chapter or heading

Encourage children to use context clues to determine the meaning of any unknown words. These strategies will help children learn to analyze the text more thoroughly as they read.

When you are finished reading this book, turn to the next-to-last page for **Text-Dependent Questions** and an **Extension Activity**.

Table of Contents

What Is Violence? 4

Stand Up Against Child Abuse 12

Kids and War 16

Top 10 Ways to Get Involved. 21

Glossary 22

Index. 23

Text-Dependent Questions 23

Extension Activity 23

About the Author. 24

What Is Violence?

Violence is when someone **physically** hurts another person on purpose. Violence can be punching, kicking, or hitting. It can be hurting someone with a weapon. Some people live with violence every day.

It is important to speak up when you see someone being violent. It doesn't matter who the violent person is. Tell a trusted adult or call 911 or another emergency number.

#ENDviolence Youth Manifesto

Nineteen-year-old Saiful Ikhwan joined 100 other kids to write the #ENDviolence Youth Manifesto. This document explains what kids around the world need to feel safe in and around their schools.

Schools do a lot to make sure students are safe from violence. Many school buildings have locked doors and windows. Kids practice safety **drills** in case of danger. Principals and teachers work hard to keep kids safe.

Make School a Safe Zone
Many schools have ways to keep strangers out. Outside doors can be locked. Video cameras can show who's at the door. Fences keep children in and strangers out. Be safe!

On Valentine's Day 2018, students at Marjory Stoneman Douglas High School heard shots. The school was under attack. Students hid inside closets and bathrooms. Most kids **survived**. One was high school senior Emma González.

Students wore shirts that said "Douglas Strong" to spread the message that they were all there for each other.

Emma got angry. She spoke out on TV about ways to keep students safe. With classmates, she helped organize March for Our Lives in Washington, DC. Between one and two million people showed up! The marchers **demanded** safer schools.

Emma González tears up as she gives a speech.

Enough Is Enough!

Emma González and over a million people chanted, "Enough is enough" as they marched. They meant that enough children have been hurt. No more!

Stand Up Against Child Abuse

It's called child **abuse** when an adult hurts a child on purpose. It can be hitting, nonstop yelling, touching that is wrong, or not paying the child enough attention. Abuse does not always show. **Victims** might stop talking, have a hard time paying attention, or seem scared.

Eleven-year-old Elijah Lee saw that a classmate had been hurt at home. Elijah said she should tell someone right away. She did, and she got help.

Elijah decided to lead a march against child abuse. He spoke to people in his hometown of Roanoke Rapids, North Carolina. He filled out papers to set up the march. Many people from his town and school all came to the march. They carried signs and marched with Elijah to **protest** child abuse. It didn't matter that he was only 11.

"Yes, I'm a kid. But kids do have a voice," Elijah said.

Elijah Lee, Superhero!

Elijah Lee was part of *Marvel's Hero Project*, a Disney+ TV show, because of his fight against child abuse. Marvel donated $10,000 to Prevent Child Abuse America. Its mission is to keep kids safe. That's just what Elijah wants!

Elijah Lee

Kids and War

It's hard to have a happy life or to pay attention in school when there is a war going on. Wars happen when two countries or groups fight each other for a long time. The war in the country of Syria started in 2011. Danger was everywhere. Some families drove to safer places. Others took trains or buses. Some walked.

Some children and their families stayed in Syria. Seven-year-old Bana al-Abed was one. Her family was trapped in the middle of the war.

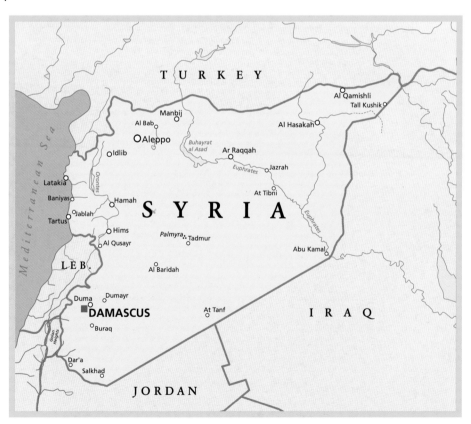

Bana al-Abed

Bana's mother opened a Twitter account for Bana. Bana tweeted almost every day to tell the world about the war. She sent photos. She showed the ruined garden where she used to play. Some days she just said, "We are still alive." Bana got people's attention. People all over the world read her tweets.

Many families who leave their homes in times of war have to stay in **refugee** camps like this one.

Then, Bana's home was threatened. She and her family had to leave Syria. Her family moved to the country of Turkey and she went back to school. Bana and her mother wrote a book. It is called *Dear World*. It tells about her time during the war. Her book asks for peace.

Just like Saiful, Emma, Elijah, and Bana, you can speak out! Join these activists and help make the world a better place!

Dear World

Syrian refugee Bana al-Abed told the world about the war she lived through. Her first tweet: "I need peace." Three years later: "I want to tell you living in peace is so nice."

Top 10 Ways to Get Involved

1 If you think someone is planning to hurt others, report it. Tell a trusted adult.

2 Help keep your school safe. Tell an adult if you see anything that could hurt students.

3 If someone hurts you or someone else, report it. Tell a trusted adult.

4 Research to find out more about issues involving violence.

5 Set an example. Solve problems between you and others with kindness.

6 Raise awareness. Organize a march or start a club against violence.

7 Write a no-violence pledge. Get other kids to sign it.

8 Join your local March for Our Lives chapter or start one at your school.

9 Collect spare change in a jar for a year. Donate it to a charity against violence.

10 Organize a fundraiser. Donate the money to a charity against violence.

Glossary

abuse (uh-BYOOS): harmful treatment of someone

demanded (di-MAN-did): asked firmly for something

drills (drilz): routines that are done over and over again

physically (FIZ-uh-kuh-lee): to do something using the body

protest (PROH-test): demonstration against something

refugee (REF-yoo-jee): a person who is forced to leave home because of war, mistreatment, or a natural disaster

survived (sur-VIVED): to have stayed alive during a dangerous event

victims (VIK-tuhmz): people who are made to suffer

Index

#ENDviolence Youth Manifesto 4
march 10, 14
Marjory Stoneman Douglas
  High School 8
safety 6

Syria 16, 20
Turkey 16, 20
violence 4, 6
Washington, DC 10

Text-Dependent Questions

1. Name four actions that are violent.
2. What should you do if you see someone being violent?
3. What should kids do right away if someone hurts them?
4. What are three ways to help keep schools safe?
5. What do many families do in times of war?

Extension Activity

One way to fight violence is to be kind. One way to be kind is to make others feel good about themselves. Make a card for someone in your class or community. On the outside, write "You matter because . . ." On the inside, write a list of things that are positive and special about that person. Decorate the card with art or colorful designs. Do not sign it. Give it anonymously.

About the Author

Chris Schwab is a writer and editor. She has written many articles for newspapers and magazines. Now she writes books for kids. She wants what Bana al-Abed wants—for every single person on the planet to have a life of peace.

Quote sources: Marvel's Hero Project, "Incredible Elijah," Disney+, November 15, 2019; account, Bana AlabedVerified. "Bana Alabed (@AlabedBana)." Twitter, September 26, 2016: https://twitter.com/AlabedBana?ref_src=twsrc%5Egoogle%7Ctwcamp%5Eserp%7Ctwgr%5Eauthor

www.rourkeeducationalmedia.com

PHOTO CREDIT: Cover, p1 ©ronniechua, ©Nikada, ©calvindexter, ©Hulinska_©Yevhenila, ©Bubushonok, ©ulimi; p5 ©quetions123; p6 ©Titikul_B; p7 ©kali9; p8 ©Jonathan Ernst/REUTERS/Newscom, p9 ©Heidi Besen, p10 ©Joseph Gruber, ©Jonathan Ernst/REUTERS/Newscom; p12 ©Pixel Memoirs; p14 ©Allies Interactive Services Pvt. Ltd.; p15 ©Les Atkins Photography; p16 ©PeterHermesFurian; p17 ©ART production; p18 ©By Orlok; p19 ©Matrix; p20 ©By answer5.

Edited by: Hailey Scragg
Cover and interior layout by: Kathy Walsh and Morgan Burnside

Library of Congress PCN Data

Kids Speak Out About Violence / Chris Schwab
(Kids Speak Out)
ISBN 978-1-73163-855-7 (hard cover)(alk. paper)
ISBN 978-1-73163-932-5 (soft cover)
ISBN 978-1-73164-009-3 (e-Book)
ISBN 978-1-73164-086-4 (ePub)
Library of Congress Control Number: 2020930055

Rourke Educational Media
Printed in the United States of America
01-1942011937